BIG DOGS & PUPPY
FACTS FOR KIDS

DOGS BOOK FOR CHILDREN
CHILDREN'S DOG BOOKS

petsunchained
(PETS & ANIMALS)

Speedy Publishing LLC

40 E. Main St. #1156

Newark, DE 19711

www.speedypublishing.com

Copyright 2017

In this book, we're going to talk about dog and puppy facts. So, let's get right to it!

FACTS ABOUT DOGS

FACT 1

Your dog has a much more sensitive sense of smell than you do. In fact, a dog's ability to smell is about a thousand times better than a human's ability to smell. Dogs have over 200-300 million scent glands compared to the 5 million that humans have.

FACT 2

Dogs also hear better than people do. They hear about ten times better.

FACT 3

When dogs are frightened, they sometimes position their tails in between their back legs. The reason for this is because they want to hinder access to the scent glands they have on their rear ends. These scent glands give information to other dogs so they hide them.

FACT 4

Border collies, poodles, and German Shepherds are some of the most intelligent dog breeds. According to animal psychologists, intelligent dogs are about as intelligent as a 2-year-old human toddler.

FACT 5

Dogs have unique nose prints that can be used to identify them, just like a human fingerprint can identify a particular person.

Most dogs don't mind swimming at all, but there are some breeds that can't swim. Dogs that have squashy looking faces, such as pugs, can't swim because they can't regulate their breaths at the same time. Dogs that have heavy heads, such as Basset hounds, or short legs, such as Dachshunds, also have problems swimming. Bulldogs have large heads as well as squashed faces and therefore sink like stones in the water.

Dog owners think that their dogs understand the passing of time, but dogs don't understand time the way we do. Their body clocks tell them when it's time to eat and when it's time to poop.

Dogs can't see as many colors as humans can see. They see in a similar way that people with color blindness do. They can actually see more colors when the lighting is low.

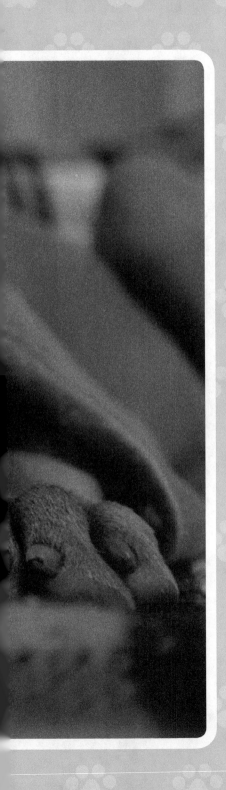

Lots of dogs, about 25%, snore when they sleep.

There are over 500 different breeds of dogs worldwide, but not all of them are officially recognized by kennel clubs.

FACT 11

Dogs don't sweat on the surface of their skin like people do. They only have sweat glands on the bottoms of their paws. They cool down by drinking lots of water and panting.

FACT 12

The shoulder blades on dogs aren't attached to the rest of their skeletons with bones. Instead, they are positioned there with ligaments as well as muscles. This gives dogs more flexibility to extend their legs when they run.

Most people have a heart rate of about 70 beats a minute. Your pet dog has a heart rate somewhere between 70 and 120 heartbeats per minute.

The tallest dog worldwide is the Great Dane and the heaviest is the St. Bernard.

Because of their enormous size, stamina, and strength, St. Bernard dogs have been very successful in assisting rescues in the mountains. A famous St. Bernard by the name of Barry saved 40 people when he worked as a rescue dog.

Dogs have been kept as pets for thousands of years. After World War II, more households in the West starting getting dogs for pets, and their popularity as pets surged in the 1960s. Today, 60% of families in the United States have a dog for a pet.

Dogs' ears can hear much higher pitch sounds than humans can hear. They can hear 8,000 Hertz compared to the upper end of human hearing at 2,000 Hertz. The famous singer from the Beatles, Paul McCartney, recorded a high-pitched whistle for his pet dog's ears in his rendition of the song "A Day in the Life." Of course, people can't hear it when they listen to the recording!

FACT 18

Three dogs that had accompanied their masters in the first class section of the Titanic, survived the sinking of the ship in 1912.

FACT 19

Scientists believe that dogs were the first animals that were domesticated. They originally came from wolves.

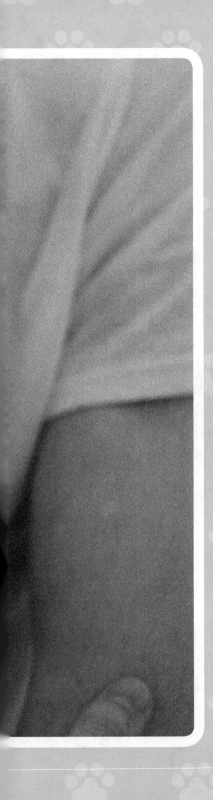

FACT

O gden Nash, the famous American poet, made the phrase describing dogs as "man's best friend" popular in the late 1900s.

FACT

L ots of dog owners, about 30%, have admitted that they talk to their pet dogs over the phone when they're out of town. Some even said they leave voice mail messages for their dogs!

FACT 22

Most dog owners, about 70%, consider their pet dog to be a member of their family. The dog's name goes on birthday and holiday cards along with the human members of the family.

The fastest dog breed in the world is the Greyhound. These sleek, graceful dogs can race up to 45 miles per hour, which is more than twice the speed of the average dog.

FACT 24

Smaller dogs live longer than larger dogs. Chihuahuas live an average of 16 years, but German Shepherds live about 10-12 years.

FACT 25

The first animal to travel in a spacecraft in orbit around Earth was a stray dog named Laika. She went up in the Soviet Sputnik 2 in the year 1957. Sadly, she died during the historic flight.

The phrase "it's raining cats and dogs" came from historical events. In the 17th century in Germany, heavy storms caused flooding and feral cats and dogs were washed into the streets with the rain and floodwaters.

Police forces and the military use German Shepherds to help in their work. German Shepherds were specifically bred to be useful in these fields since they are intelligent and not easily disturbed by the sounds of gunshots or enemy fire. They are also incredibly loyal to their masters and very courageous.

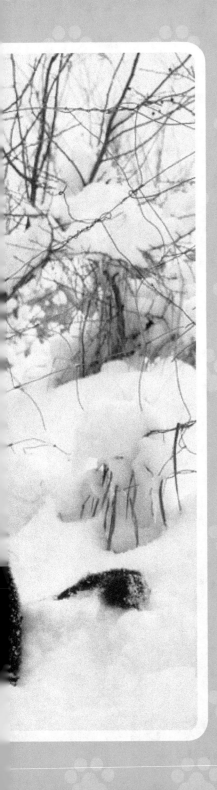

The smallest dog breed in the world is the Chihuahua. The name Chihuahua comes from the Mexican border that they crossed to get into the United States.

Newfoundland dogs were bred in Canada originally. They have very thick coats to insulate them during the cold Canadian winters and webbed feet to help them swim efficiently over large waterways.

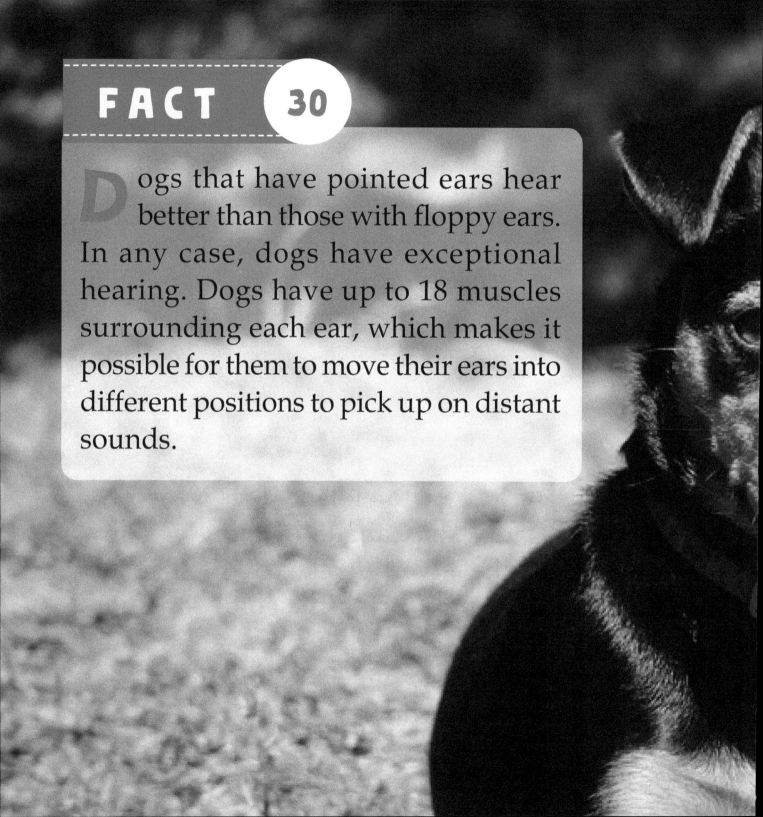

Dogs that have pointed ears hear better than those with floppy ears. In any case, dogs have exceptional hearing. Dogs have up to 18 muscles surrounding each ear, which makes it possible for them to move their ears into different positions to pick up on distant sounds.

FACTS ABOUT PUPPIES

FACT 31

Puppies have the same five senses as humans, but the first sense they use after they're born is the sense of touch.

FACT 32

If you look at a puppy's feet, you'll get a good idea how large your puppy will get when he or she is full grown. Big feet means that there's a lot of growing in the future!

FACT 33

It doesn't make any sense to give your puppy a long name. He or she will only hear the first syllable of the first word. So, if you name your pup, "Princess Messy," she'll only hear "Prin."

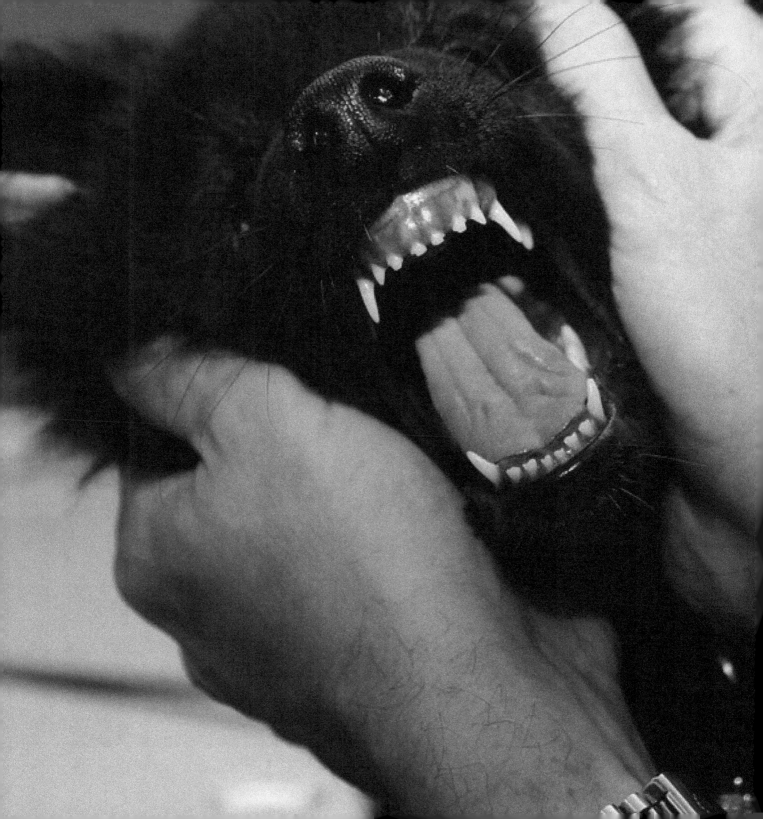

Puppies are born without any teeth! Their baby teeth grow in after they are a month old. However, they only keep those teeth for about four months and then they begin to lose them and their adult teeth grown in.

FACT 35

When puppies play with you, they might nip or bite your hand. If you just say "ouch" loudly it quickly trains them out of it. It's similar to the "yelp" they make when one of their siblings bites them.

FACT

E ven though dogs have one of the best senses of smell of any animal, when they are first born, they can't smell at all! Their scent glands don't develop until they reach about three weeks old.

FACT 37

Don't show your teeth when you're smiling at your puppy! Teeth mean that you're about to attack them or that you're aggressive.

fter they are born, it takes a while for puppies to get used to staying awake. Their first week they are only awake about 10% of the time and asleep 90% of the time. When they become adults, they'll need about 10 hours of daily sleep.

Sometimes if puppies are born by caesarean section, their mother doesn't recognize them if they are cleaned before they get close to her. That's because the mother dog, called a dam, uses her sense of smell to recognize her puppies.

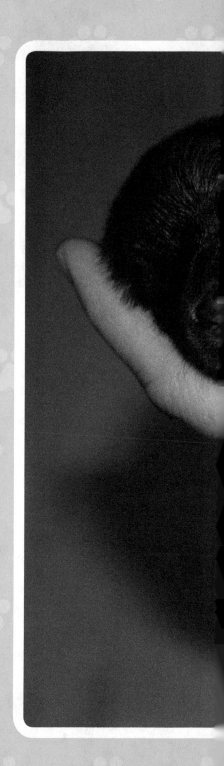

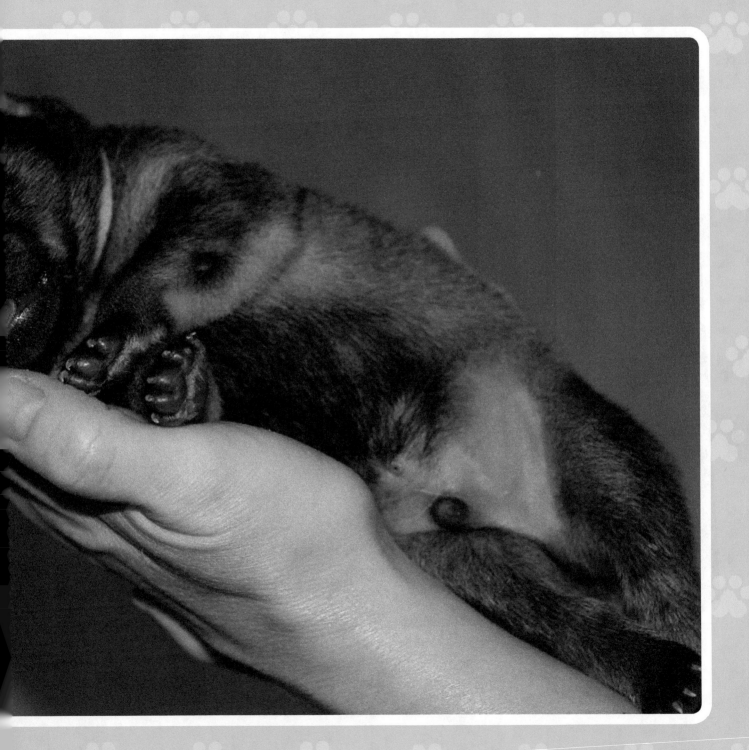

A DOG IS A MAN'S BEST FRIEND

Dogs were domesticated from wolves thousands of years ago. It's believed that they were the very first domesticated animals. Today there are hundreds of different breeds of dogs to choose from if you're getting a pet. Sixty percent of American families own a dog and believe that their pet dog is "man's best friend."

Awesome! Now that you've read fun facts about dogs and puppies you may want to read about German Shepherd dogs in the Pets Unchained book *Woof! Woof! Bark! Bark! | German Shepherd Dog Book for Kids | Children's Dog Books.*

Printed in the USA
CPSIA information can be obtained
at www.ICGtesting.com
LVHW070712241123
764802LV00016B/844